Silk, Sand and Sea

Silk, Sand and Sea

Anita Ganeri
Illustrated by **Pino Cao**

Collins

Intrepid traveller

More than 750 years ago, a young man called Marco Polo set off from his home in Venice, Italy, on an unforgettable journey to East Asia. He returned, more than 20 years later, having travelled to China and back, and after the adventure of many lifetimes. He was bursting with stories about what he'd seen, and he couldn't wait to share them with anyone prepared to listen. To European ears, many of the sights and sounds he described sounded much too far-fetched to be true, but Marco knew what he'd seen and heard. To the end of his life, he never got tired of telling his tales, whether people believed them or not.

This is Marco's astonishing story, as he himself might have told it ...

1. Early life

I was born in the city of Venice, Italy, in the year 1254. I don't know the exact date – we're not big on birthdays in my family. For many years, I was sure I was an orphan – I had never met my father, and my mother died when I was very young. Sadly, I don't remember much about her, although I'm told she was very beautiful and kind. Fortunately, I come from a large family, and my aunt and uncle took me in after my mother's death. I went to live with them and my cousins in their big, old house, down by the main canal.

Of course, I missed my mother – and I wish she could see me now – but there wasn't time to feel lonely or sad. Our household was always busy, with visitors coming and going at all times of the day, so I had plenty of company. I spent my whole childhood here in Venice – it's the best place in the world to grow up (though I'd never actually been anywhere else at that time).

Like most Venetians, my family were merchants, trading in precious jewels, silks, spices and other luxury goods from all over the world. By the time I was born, business was booming, and my family had become wealthy, even by Venice's standards. We lived very comfortably and had everything we could possibly need. Better still – reputation is everything in Venice – the Polo name had become well known and respected around the city. As a boy, I was desperate to follow in my family's footsteps and become a merchant. I was taught mathematics and book-keeping and was quick at learning languages, but I regularly skipped school and spent the day listening to the adults talking business and learning the tricks of the trade.

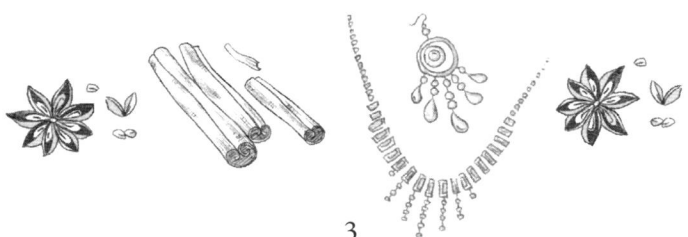

At the time, Venice was one of the world's most important cities for trade. Every day, merchants came and went from all over the world, and the harbour was packed with huge **galleys**. I spent hours down by the docks, watching the sailors and their exotic cargoes – luxuries like silk, ivory, ostrich feathers, pearls, gold dust, salt, sandalwood and pomegranates. I'd never seen anything like it before. It made me even more determined to one day travel to the far-flung places they came from – I spent hours daydreaming about this, to my aunt's dismay. Then, one day, when I was 15 years old, a ship arrived in Venice that changed everything for me.

It started off like any other day. I sneaked out of the house and down to the harbour to watch the latest arrivals. When two men, dressed in flowing robes, disembarked from one of the ships, I thought their faces looked vaguely familiar, but didn't pay them much attention. And when I looked at them properly, I knew I hadn't ever seen them before. It was probably a good job I didn't know what lay in store because, when I discovered who the strangers were, I got the shock of my life.

They were none other than my father, Niccolò, and uncle, Maffeo. I couldn't believe my eyes. Sixteen years after leaving Venice on a trading trip to East Asia, they were back. I was born a few months after they went, by which time they were thousands of kilometres away. So, I'd never met my father, and he had no idea he had a son. When we were finally introduced, I don't know who got the bigger surprise.

With my father at home, things began to change, to put it mildly. It turned my world upside down! The first thing was to try to get to know each other, but neither of us was much good at small talk. So, I asked him about his trip instead and, boy, what an extraordinary trip it had been. He was obviously keen to talk about it – in fact, once he got started, he was difficult to stop. I didn't mind a bit. I was fascinated by his stories and never got tired of hearing them. The things he'd seen and done were awesome and almost unbelievable, even though he swore he was telling the truth. I mean, what reason did he have to make it up? Here's a shortened version of what he told me.

The brothers left Venice by sea and immediately regretted it. Conditions on board were appalling – the ship was filthy, overcrowded and swarming with cockroaches and rats. Life was made more miserable, if that was possible, by the overpowering stench of rotting food and human waste. By the time they reached **Constantinople**, Turkey, a few weeks later, they hoped never to set foot on a ship again. So, after hiring camels and horses, they continued their journey overland, following a network of trade routes, known as the **Silk Road**. Ahead of them stretched the vast Mongol Empire.

Back in Europe, we knew the Mongols to be brutal warriors who'd taken control of most of Asia, leaving a trail of devastation behind. Surely, I asked my father, it was less risky to turn around and head back home? Quite the opposite, he replied. In fact, the deeper they ventured into Mongol lands, the safer they felt, thanks to none other than the Mongol emperor, Hulagu Khan. Keen to encourage European traders to visit, he declared a truce allowing them to travel safely across the empire.

Rather than being scared off by the Mongols' terrifying reputation, my father and uncle threw themselves wholeheartedly into Mongol life. It was the best way of winning them around, they reckoned. They wore Mongol clothing, spoke Mongolian, and slept in large, round Mongol tents, called *gers*. They even gave up washing, according to Mongol custom, despite the terrible smell in the ger.

Desperate not to cause offence, they also tried *koumiss*, fermented horse milk, the Mongols' favourite drink. If it sounded dreadful, it tasted even worse, my father told me; especially as the Mongols kept pulling his ears while he was drinking to force him to take a good, long gulp!

Anyway, so far, so good, and when they reached the city of Bukhara, they had another stroke of luck. The city was packed with merchants from Europe and Asia and, with so much business to do, they stayed longer than expected. There was also some local unrest, which made it difficult for them to leave. By chance, they met a Mongol official who was on his way back to China to deliver a report to the new emperor, Kublai Khan (Hulagu Khan's brother). Greatly impressed by the brothers, he suggested they travel with him so he could introduce them to the emperor. It was an offer they couldn't refuse, even though it meant another gruelling year on the road until they finally reached **Cambulac**, and Kublai Khan's winter palace.

Meeting the most powerful man alive took them by surprise. He was polite, clever, curious and welcoming. He bombarded them with questions about life in Europe and, in particular, Christianity. My father and uncle answered as best they could – in almost fluent Mongolian, to the **khan**'s enormous delight. In fact, the three of them got on so well, my father and uncle stayed at the Mongol court for many years.

When the time finally came for them to leave, the emperor entrusted them with a special mission. They were to deliver a letter from him to the Pope in **Acre** in the **Holy Land**, asking for 100 priests to teach him and his people more about Christianity. The brothers were to accompany the priests back to China, and also bring holy oil from the temple in Jerusalem. The oil was said to have healing powers. Before they left, the emperor gave them gold tablets, called *paiza*, stamped with his **royal seal**. These guaranteed safe passage through his empire.

My father and uncle were keen to deliver the letter and fetch the oil, and set off immediately. But when they arrived in Acre in 1269, their plans were thrown into chaos. The old pope had died and, until a new one was elected, they couldn't go anywhere. While they waited, they decided to slip back to Venice for a quick visit, which is when I first met them – little did they know, they'd be there for two whole years.

The waiting around made my father furious. He'd grown used to life on the move and couldn't bear being stuck in one place. He frequently lost his temper, and everyone was relieved when a new pope was announced, and he and my uncle could get back on the road. They would be retracing their previous route to China, but with an extra travelling companion this time. I was going with them! Yes, me, Marco Polo! I couldn't believe my luck. I was going to meet Kublai Khan, at last, and even though it meant leaving home for the first time, I was so excited, I forgot to be nervous.

2. Goodbye, Venice

We left Venice on a fine spring day in 1271 – I had no idea when, or even if, I'd see the city again. Still, feeling homesick wasn't going to help. I needed all my energy for what lay ahead, and, to be honest, I was more worried about being seasick. We boarded a ship heading south-east to Acre and made our way slowly along the coast, stopping here and there to take on supplies. Apart from the three of us, most of the passengers were Christian pilgrims on their way to the Holy Land. Already, I found myself surrounded by so many new sights and sounds. It was pretty overwhelming but at least it was a distraction from those pesky rats.

Acre is an ancient city on the Mediterranean Sea, famous for its towering walls. It's a stopping-off point for pilgrims, and they were packed into the tiny port. I'd have loved a good look around but, of course, my father and uncle had been here before and already seen the sights. So, we joined the pilgrims on their way to Jerusalem, collected the holy oil, then headed straight back to Acre. As luck would have it, the new pope was an old friend of my father and uncle and gladly read the letter from Kublai Khan. He offered the services of two of his most trusted priests (I know, it wasn't quite the hundred the khan hoped for) and sent them on their way with a letter to the khan, jewels and other gifts for the emperor.

We left Acre in high spirits and headed east, at last! Even though my father and uncle were used to travelling, the going would be seriously tough, for me especially. At least we had Kublai Khan's paiza to protect us along the Silk Road. We'd need them where we were going. Things took a turn for the worse only too quickly, when we were crossing Armenia. I've no idea why but the local ruler took an instant dislike to us and threatened to throw us into prison if we didn't leave. That was also when the two priests ran away, frightened for their lives. We let them go and carried on. Despite the risks, we'd come too far to turn back now. The plan now was to make our way south by camel and on foot to the port city of **Hormuz** on the Persian Gulf. From there, we'd board a ship and sail to India, and beyond that, to China.

After leaving Armenia, we crossed Turkey and then Iraq. There was so much to take in. Every day brought new sights and sounds, languages, food and customs. But I was slowly getting used to life on the road, though I often dreamt of our house in Venice and, especially, my oh-so-comfortable bed. I planned to jot down notes about all the places we visited so I wouldn't forget anything, and where better than **Tauris** in Iran to start?

It was such a beautiful place, surrounded by sumptuous orchards and with bustling markets selling goods from all over the world. But the best thing, by far, was the pearls. In Tauris, bartering for pearls is a serious business.

Buyer and seller sit facing each other, their hands hidden under a cloth. They don't say anything out loud, to avoid being overheard. Instead, they haggle over prices by squeezing each other's fingers in certain ways. I couldn't wait to try this in Venice – imagine the look on people's faces!

From Tauris, we trudged through a desperately dry desert to the city of Kerman, famous for its exquisite Persian rugs. I'd have loved to buy one to take home. For the first time in weeks, the weather was good, and I spent a happy few days exploring the mountains and admiring the falcons (my favourite birds) and other wildlife. Next came a long, tedious ride through the countryside with no sign of any villages or towns. The only people around were **nomads** roaming the region with their cattle and sheep.

Speaking of cattle … high in the mountains, we came across herds of snow-white oxen – an extraordinary sight. They had short hair, stumpy horns, large humps and gentle natures and, despite their great size, seemed surprisingly easy to handle. They lay down for their owners to tie sacks and bags to their backs, then stood up again once they were fully loaded. Clever, eh? While there was clearly nothing to fear from the oxen, the region's bandits were another thing. They preyed on nomads' animals and had the power to turn day into night so they could hunt under cover of darkness. At least, that's what local legend said. There was no escape from their bloodthirsty ways, and we weren't about to hang around to see. As fast as we could, we hurried on our way to Hormuz, our last stop before India.

Our stay in this bustling city started off well enough. Everywhere we went, we came across Indian merchants selling spices, pearls, silk and elephant ivory. It was fascinating to watch but I wish someone had warned us about the wind. It's so horribly hot and dry, it can prove deadly unless you dive into cold water immediately, and that's not easy to do here. As for the ship we'd hired to take us to India and then to China …

After so many days of desert, we were looking forward to being back at sea, but the ship was in a terrible state. There were so many things wrong with it, it's difficult to know where to start. Instead of nails, the planks were held together by wooden pegs and coconut-shell thread. It had only one mast and one sail, which would surely make it unstable in stormy weather. There wasn't a deck to speak of, just animal skins stretched to cover the cargo. Worst of all, the timbers were coated with fish oil, yes, fish oil, in place of tar, to make them waterproof. If we set out in this leaky wreck, we'd sink – I was sure of it. So, we had to rethink our travel plans. Abandoning the idea of sailing south to India, we decided to head north and go overland instead. We'd ride along the Silk Road on donkeys and camels, just as generations of merchants had done before us. What could possibly go wrong?

3. Walking with ghosts

I spoke too soon. Almost immediately things went horribly wrong. I blame the camels – nasty beasts. They're the two-humped kind with massive teeth – they're called Bactrian camels, I think. They're brilliantly suited to desert life, with broad, hairy hooves so they don't sink into the sand, and large, hairy nostrils they close to keep the sand out. They can also go for days without water and, admittedly, that's a pretty handy skill to have. But the wretched creatures are also serious spitters and sway as they walk. After a few days in the saddle, you ache so much you can barely stand up. Trouble is, they're by far the best transport around, so we didn't have a choice (and anyway, pesky donkeys were almost as bad).

We had to go back to Kerman to join our camel caravan, then it was back across the desert once more. My fellow travellers seemed decent enough but it's the safety in numbers that counts. At night, we stayed at the nearest **caravanserai** – they were usually located in an **oasis**, which came as a relief. The buildings weren't much to look at from the outside – just a high wall with air holes at the bottom and small windows at the top, complete with massive gates. They looked more like prisons than places you'd pick to stop for a nap.

Once inside, though, they usually got better, I'm glad to say. In the centre was a shady courtyard with splashing fountains, surrounded by storerooms and stables. Narrow stairways led up to rooms for the guests. It's true, the rooms were small, bare and draughty, but at least they didn't sway (or spit). Below the rooms, there were stables for the animals, so the camels also got a good rest.

The journey across the desert was dreadful. Worse than dreadful. There was nothing to drink, not a drop of clean water, which is fine if you're a camel but torture for anyone else.

By the time, we reached the next oasis, we were almost fainting from thirst. Luckily, this particular oasis was famous for melons. I gobbled quite a few down and can safely say I've never tasted anything so delicious in all my life. When we left, I made sure to load my camel up with plenty for the trip. Our next stop was Afghanistan. At first, the countryside we rode through was beautiful – lush, green valleys and mountain slopes, covered in almond trees.

It cheered me up no end, despite the constant, eye-watering smell of camel.

Sadly, this gorgeous scenery soon gave way to dry, dusty wasteland again, so you can imagine how glad we were to eventually reach a city famous for stunning rubies and sapphires, mined in the nearby mountains. My father and uncle were ecstatic! They couldn't wait to trade gold and gems for these precious stones – it's the happiest I've seen them in weeks. For safekeeping, we sewed the jewels we bought into the linings of our cloaks and made sure we never let our cloaks out of our sight. You never know where robbers are lurking and it pays to be careful, especially when the jewels are worth a small fortune.

(Quite a long time) Later …

Well, we're still here in the city, I'm afraid. You see, around a year ago, I fell ill with a cough and a fever and had to spend months in bed. It was probably due to all that travelling. You don't say! I hated being cooped up inside and, as soon as I felt strong enough, I started going for short walks in the mountains around the city. It was so beautiful up there and being in the pure, clean air was bliss; not to mention the wonders it did for my health. The doctors were amazed with my progress – within just a few weeks, I felt like my old self again. My father and uncle were delighted. Naturally, they'd been worried about me and made sure I got plenty of rest, but we were now a whole year behind schedule, and they were desperate to get going again.

So, it was back to the Silk Road, and back on a camel, and it was like we'd never been away. We were heading into the **Pamir Mountains**, but first, we had a long, treacherous trek upriver. Boy, it was hard going – the higher we went, the steeper the trail. It was also getting colder – I suppose all those snow-capped peaks were a clue – and harder to breathe in the **thinning air**. Even the birds had given up and flown off somewhere else. All the time we were in the mountains, I didn't spot a single one. How our camels kept their footing, I'll never know. With sheer drops on either side of the path, it only needed one false step, and we'd have all been dead.

Good old camels (I'm trying to be more positive about them!) For my part, I was so scared, I hardly dared look down and, for about the millionth time since we left Venice, I asked myself what on earth I was doing.

Fortunately, things got better around the next bend. We crossed a vast open plain between two towering mountain peaks. It was a picture-perfect scene – lush, green grass, gleaming lakes and a raging, rushing river with wild sheep dotted all around. But we didn't dare linger in this idyllic-looking place for long. At night, local people warned us, hungry wolves ventured down from the slopes to kill sheep. We needed to be on our way before night fell but when we rejoined the track, the way ahead was marked with piles of animal bones, a grisly memento left behind by earlier travellers.

I can't tell you how relieved I was to reach the oasis town of **Khotan** on the edge of the desert. OK, so we were still in the middle of nowhere but at least the people were welcoming and there were crops like cotton, flax, wheat and corn growing in the fields. Compared to where we'd come from, it was a safe place, but we only had time for a short rest. With so much lost time to make up, we stocked up on supplies, loaded our camels and pushed on east again. I wish we'd never left.

A few days later, we arrived in the city of **Lop**, our starting point for the gruelling Gobi Desert. Back in Khotan, people warned us to take everything with us we'd need for a month. That's how long it took to get across the desert, and there was nothing to eat or drink once you were in there. I wanted to believe they were exaggerating – after all the deserts we'd trudged through on this trip, surely this desert couldn't be worse.

But it was – much, much worse. As far as the eye could see, there was nothing but stretch after endless stretch of gravel and sand. The weather was unbearable – freezing cold nights and baking hot days, with wind that never stopped howling. It blew so fiercely, it swept the ground bare of sand, blasting it against the rocks – and into our eyes, noses and clothes. I seriously doubted we'd ever get out of this place alive.

Everything was far
worse at night. I'd
heard stories about
desert ghosts tricking travellers
into leaving their companions and
getting hopelessly lost. I really hoped they were
just that – stories. Then, I began hearing voices
calling me to follow, along with the sound of
drums and harps being played. Sometimes, a
loud hum accompanied the voices; sometimes,

a loud shrieking sound. I don't suppose anyone will believe this at home – they'll say I've been out in the sun for too long. To reduce the risk, I stuck close to my father and uncle and we hung bells around our camels' necks. These were tricks I'd learnt from other travellers, otherwise I'd probably never have been heard of again.

After the worst few weeks of my life, we finally emerged, only barely alive, from the wretched desert. We'd reached the province of Tangut in China – a very long way from home. We'd already been on the road for three years – surely, we were nearly there? Wishful thinking, sadly. We still had more than 3,000 kilometres to go to Kublai Khan's court – I could hardly bear to think about it, and it wasn't just me suffering. I admit it – by now I'd grown quite fond of my camel, but we were both exhausted.

4. Meeting Kublai Khan

To take my mind off the aches and pains, I made pages and pages of notes about the unusual and wonderful sights I saw. There were plenty of them, I can tell you. Once, as we were setting off across yet another dreadful desert, we came to a mountain that was famous for its "salamander". Back home, people believed salamanders were animals that fire couldn't burn but that's nonsense. Salamander is actually a material mined from the mountainside, then twisted into threads, like wool. The threads are dried in the sun, pounded in a mortar and carefully washed, then woven into cloth. But this is no ordinary cloth – it's worth the same as gold. No wonder it's mostly used for burying kings and high-ranking nobles.

Even though we were travelling at more of a snail's than a camel's pace, we were slowly getting closer to Cambulac, the city in which Kublai Khan spent the winter months. Travelling such long distances every day, I appreciated just how vast his empire was. It was founded by **Genghis Khan** – a name guaranteed to strike fear into people's hearts back home. I decided to give him the benefit of the doubt. After all, Genghis Khan was Kublai Khan's grandfather, so I reckoned he couldn't have been all bad. I'd come to admire the Mongols for their toughness and skill in battle, and I quickly took to their way of life.

There were some things I really enjoyed. Sleeping in a ger took some getting used to, but now I don't think twice about it. Besides, gers are brilliantly practical when you're on the move. They're constructed from wooden poles, made into a frame and covered in felt, and are cleverly designed to be quick to take down and sling on a cart, and quick to put up again.

I also got hooked on falconry – Mongol falcons were the finest I'd ever seen.

They're used to catch rabbits and other animals for the cooking pot. Now, rabbit I could manage – we often ate it in Venice – but the Mongols were also partial to horse, camel and dog. Acquiring a taste for these took longer but, in the end, you'll eat anything if you're hungry enough. Well, almost anything. They're also fond of a kind of soup, called *borbi*, which they make by boiling sheep's bones in a bucket of water. It's the most disgusting thing I've ever tasted and I'd have to be starving to even think about eating it. Then, there was koumiss – remember, I told you about it? The Mongols loved it so much, it's almost all they drank.

Even though refusing a cup of koumiss is viewed as an insult, I carried on doing it as long as I dared. I gave in, eventually, and besides, sharing koumiss around is much more than a way of quenching your thirst. It was the way Mongol warriors bonded, and I must say, it did the trick – they always supported each other. And anyway, if you can cope with a diet of koumiss and camel, I think you can cope with almost anything else.

Finally, four gruelling years after leaving Venice, we reached Cambulac. I know, I could hardly believe it either. On the way, we'd almost frozen to death, died of thirst, and been terrified by ghostly voices, so it was a miracle we'd made it alive. As soon as our arrival was announced, everything happened in a bit of a blur. We were summoned to the main hall of the palace where we were given soft leather slippers to wear. When I looked puzzled, my father told me it was because the floor was covered in the finest silk carpets, and our outdoors shoes would have left dirty marks.

Kublai Khan sat on his throne at the far end of the room, surrounded by his barons. My hero, at last.

Smiling, he beckoned my father and uncle forward and they knelt before him. They stayed like that for minutes that felt like hours, until the emperor ordered them to their feet and warmly welcomed them back to court. It was clear how delighted he was to see his old friends again. He asked them about their journey, and he was astonished at the hardships they'd been through. In turn, my father and uncle replied that it was all worth it for finding the emperor in such excellent health. They'd long ago learnt how to flatter the khan!

But now they had something for him, they said and, without further delay, they handed over the Pope's letter carried all the way from Acre. Kublai Khan was thrilled. That left one last gift to present to the khan – the holy oil from Jerusalem. The emperor declared it the most precious thing he'd ever been given and ordered his most trusted guards to keep it safe.

And then, it was my turn ... I'd been waiting nearby for my father to present me to the emperor. My legs turned to jelly – I don't know how I didn't collapse in a heap on the floor. I was so starstruck I could hardly breathe. They say you shouldn't meet your heroes, in case you're disappointed. But Kublai Khan was everything I'd hoped for, and here was the most powerful ruler on Earth telling *me* how pleased he was to meet me! Never mind the nightmare to get here; this was the greatest day of my whole life.

Over the years that followed, I got to know the khan and his family very well. I was particularly fond of his wife, Chabi, who was always on hand to give the khan wise and sensible advice. I knew what people back home thought of him, but I have nothing but good things to report. It can't have been easy having Genghis Khan as your grandfather, but Kublai Khan didn't rely on those family ties. He was smart, brave and cunning – excellent qualities for any ruler.

As soon as he'd become emperor, he'd set about putting his own stamp on the empire. One thing he did was order merchants to use paper money instead of their usual metal coins. In Venice, we'd always reckoned paper money wasn't, well, worth the paper it was written on, but the khan had other ideas. At the royal mint at Cambulac, he had notes printed on paper made from the bark of mulberry trees. The paper was cut into squares, each worth a different amount of money, stamped with the royal seal and marked so it couldn't be forged. If stocks ran low, it didn't matter – the emperor simply printed some more. Genius, I thought.

Under Kublai Khan, the Mongol Empire quickly expanded and grew fantastically rich. It helped that, from early on, he wisely involved people from the places he ruled over to help him to run things. He was also keen to welcome merchants, artists and craftspeople from far and wide to court. I particularly admired the way he looked after his people – and that's another thing they won't believe back home. If the harvest was good, he put aside tonnes of grain to give away if famine struck later. He regularly handed out new clothes, made by tailors as part of their duty to him. And that wasn't all: every morning, crowds of poor people could be seen queuing patiently at the palace gates, waiting for their daily loaf of bread from the emperor. For many of them, this was the only thing standing between them and starvation.

For my part, my stay in Cambulac felt like the most fantastic dream you could ever have. I had to pinch myself every day to remind myself it was actually happening. I mean, how lucky was I? The city was beautiful, and the khan's palace astonishingly grand. To enter, you climbed up a monumental marble staircase – there was one on either side of the doors.

Inside, every inch of wall and ceiling was covered in shimmering silver and gold, as well as exquisite paintings of birds and animals. However many times I saw it, it always took my breath away. The main hall was enormous, with room for more than 6,000 people, and I lost count of how many other rooms the palace had. At the back were the emperor's private apartments, along with closely-guarded storerooms for his treasure. Surrounding the palace were two sets of high white walls, with beautiful parks, lakes and a hill, called Green Mount, in between. Green Mount was built from soil dug out of the lake and was where Kublai Khan had his favourite trees carried up by elephant and planted.

Without doubt, the highlight of the year at court was Kublai Khan's birthday in September. For the celebrations, the khan and his thousands of barons dressed in stunning robes of beaten gold and silk, decorated with gleaming jewels and shimmering pearls.

The barons, of course, were careful not to outshine the emperor – it was more than their lives were worth. I must admit feeling jealous of all the fuss – I didn't even know when the actual date of my birthday was.

Another spectacular event took place in February to mark the New Year. It was called the "White Festival" because everyone dressed in white, a lucky colour. During the day, a procession of elephants, draped in fabulous white cloth and carrying caskets filled with gifts, filed majestically past the khan. Other gifts poured into the palace from all over the empire, many of them white to bring the emperor good luck. One year, I was told, he was given 100,000 white horses – now that's the sort of gift I'd like. A sumptuous banquet rounded off an extraordinary day, where the fortunate guests were entertained by the finest jugglers and acrobats found in the empire.

5. Ambassador Polo

From the start, the emperor and I got on brilliantly – even my father and uncle remarked on how highly he always spoke of me. I reckon he was flattered by how quickly I'd taken to Mongol life – you see, all those years on the road hadn't been wasted. By now, I could speak Mongolian fluently, along with several other languages. I don't mean to boast but I even impressed myself. Anyway, whatever the reason, I quickly became a trusted member of his court.

Not everyone was pleased. The barons complained about favouritism and how I was getting too big for my boots. But what did they know? They were just jealous at how clever and popular I was and really had nothing to moan about. Kublai Khan rewarded their loyalty with generous gifts of gold, silver and jewels. There were also special grades of paiza – silver for a baron who commanded 100 warriors; gold for 1,000; gold with a lion's head for 10,000; and gold with lions, falcons, the sun and moon for 100,000 men. This last one was the highest honour in the whole empire. Never mind worrying about me, they should have counted themselves lucky.

I hadn't a clue how long we'd be staying at court, but I knew my father and uncle wanted to get back to Venice as soon as they possibly could. It wasn't going to be easy to leave, however. We needed the emperor's permission, and he wasn't about to let us go. As for me, most of the time, I was happy exploring the city and running errands for the khan, but I soon found I needed something else to fill my days. Be careful what you wish for!

One day, out of the blue, Kublai Khan summoned me and offered me a job I couldn't refuse. He was appointing me as his ambassador to collect taxes (and secret information) from every corner of the empire – it seemed my travelling days weren't over yet! For this, my languages would come in very useful, but I was worried – I was in my early twenties by then and had never had a proper job in my life. Also, I'd never travelled anywhere on my own – believe it or not – and my father and uncle weren't coming with me this time. I'd just have to do my best. And, as I kept reminding myself, it was a great honour to be working for the khan.

My first mission was to a city about six months' ride from Cambulac. Not wanting to leave anything to chance, I spent days preparing for the trip beforehand. I wanted to show up those sniping barons by becoming the best ambassador Kublai Khan had ever had. I'm pleased to say the trip was a great success and the emperor was delighted with my report. It was strange being back on the road again, but travelling in the emperor's service was a very different experience from the one I'd had. For one thing, the roads themselves were well kept and well signposted, and for another, excellent lodgings were provided at regular intervals with a supply of fresh horses for the next day's ride. After what I'd been used to, it was the height of luxury, and I was eternally grateful for that.

This trip turned out to be the first of many journeys I made for Kublai Khan. For the next 20 years – yes, 20 years – I travelled the length and breadth of the Mongol Empire, criss-crossing China and far beyond. I did my best to keep records of everywhere I went and everything I saw. But I visited so many places they often merged into each other, and I most likely missed things out. These are a few of the highlights of my trips, though not necessarily in the right order.

The emperor must have been pleased with me because he sent me to **Quinsay** next. At the time, it was the biggest, richest, most fabulous city in China and, of all the hundreds of places I visited, Quinsay was my favourite. Nothing I write about this glorious place will do it justice, so bear with me while I try. Quinsay and Cambulac were linked by a colossal canal (nothing in Venice comes close). All I could do was admire this incredible feat of engineering. I followed it for most of the way, marvelling at the sights I passed – stunning bridges with tall pillars, topped with marble lions; lush, green fields and bustling villages and Buddhist monasteries where the monks were busy making silk.

Speaking of silk-making … did you know silk was invented in China and was kept top secret for centuries? Silk was so valuable, that only the emperor and his family could afford to wear it. Incredibly, it all begins with little silkworms (strictly speaking, not worms at all but silk moth caterpillars). What happens is this … silk moths lay their eggs in mulberry trees and the silkworms that hatch out of the eggs feast on mulberry leaves. When it's time for them to transform into adult moths, they spin fluffy white cocoons around themselves. The cocoons are picked and dunked in boiling water, where they unravel into silk threads.

This doesn't sound great for the silkworms, I know, but I'm not giving up my silk robe, however cruel it is.

Getting back to Quinsay, it wasn't called the City of Heaven for nothing – it truly was a heavenly place. Sitting against a backdrop of dreamy mountains, it was built, like Venice, around a network of canals where boats of all shapes and sizes jostled for space. I felt at home at once! And the best thing was, despite the area being taken over by the Mongols, its magnificent buildings and wonderful way of life had mostly been left untouched.

On one side of the city was a crystal-clear lake; on the other an enormous river. There must have been thousands of bridges – I couldn't count them all – the largest so high, a tall ship with a mast could pass underneath, while horses and carriages clattered overhead. The city itself was vast and sprawling – and more crowded than anywhere else I'd been. It was particularly busy on market days when I joined shoppers to browse the stalls heaving with fresh fruit and vegetables, and fish from the sea.

It took me a while to win people's trust – I was representing the Mongol emperor, after all. I told them the Mongols could only dream of living like them. My only regret was never getting the hang of Chinese languages, despite my way with words. On my walks around the city, I met merchants, grown rich on trade, living in splendid houses, together with all kinds of craftspeople, painters, actors, poets and writers. People worked hard but they also liked to enjoy themselves. In the late afternoon, they made their way home to spend the rest of the day writing poetry, playing chess or going boating. If they got hungry at any time, some of the city's noodle shops stayed open all night.

One of the things I liked most on my travels was seeing so many amazing animals and birds that were completely new to me. But I quickly learnt not to get too close – just in case they weren't friendly to humans. Countless dangerously hungry beasts roamed the countryside, on the hunt for food. In Tibet, I heard about vicious stripy cats that preyed on unwary travellers – it sent shivers down my spine. Fortunately, I didn't see any, but one night, as I was dropping off to sleep, I got the fright of my life. An ear-splitting sound tore through the darkness. Pop! Pop! Pop! Pop! It was so loud, I was terrified.

Next morning, I found out what it was. To scare off hungry wild cats, local people burnt cartloads of canes, and as the canes twisted and split in the fire, they made the dreadful din I'd heard. While I'm on the subject of wild cats, here's another tip from the jungles of Vietnam. There, the stripy cats usually stay out of sight, but you can hear their howling all day and all night. Our local guides warned us against sleeping outside so we made our beds in small boats in the middle of the river, hopefully too far from the shore for the wild cats to swim to. It worked and I wasn't eaten, though I don't think I got a single wink of sleep.

6. Heading home

The years flew by and, for a long time, with Kublai Khan at the height of his powers, all seemed well in the empire. Then disaster struck. The emperor's beloved wife, Chabi, died suddenly, and things took a terrible turn. Stricken with grief, it wasn't long before the khan's health, too, began to go downhill. What's more, without Chabi's wise advice to guide him, he started to lose his grip on the empire he'd worked so hard to build up. Rumours spread like wildfire around court about what might happen next.

The khan had always been stubborn, but now he refused to listen to anyone. He made one bad decision after another, including launching an attack on Japan.

Everyone knew such an invasion would fail, and it did, spectacularly. On land, the Mongols were brilliant warriors, but at sea it was a different story, and Japan was made up of numerous islands. This disastrous defeat marked a humiliating turning point for the emperor, and he was never the same again. He wasn't the only one in turmoil – his subjects felt it, too. Before this, the Mongols had a reputation for being unbeatable. Now, they no longer had the power to strike fear in people's hearts.

Back at court, Kublai Khan blamed everyone but himself for the terrible state he found himself in. With his empire collapsing around him, he shut himself away in his rooms and spent his days **gorging** on huge quantities of rich food and koumiss. As the weeks passed, he grew more unhappy. For those of us who loved and admired the khan, it was very sad to see – before our eyes, he had turned from an all-conquering hero into a weak and broken old man.

For my father, my uncle and me, the khan's decline also marked a change in our fortunes.

For as long as we'd been in China, the emperor had looked after us and kept us safe. But if he died, and it surely wouldn't be long the way he was going, we'd lose all our hard-won protection and privileges. One thing was certain – we needed to think about going home. But first, I had a trip to India to plan. I'd wanted to go there for ages, and this was most probably my last chance. I sailed on one of the great merchant ships that come and go between China and India. It was amazing to be back on the water again. And what fine ships they were – this one had 60 luxury cabins!

During the voyage, I called in on some of the islands and kingdoms of Indonesia where people kept me entertained with their tales of unicorns. These beasts had huge feet, horns in the middle of their foreheads, and long, sharp spines on their teeth – a far cry from the mythical creatures we were so fond of back home. In Sri Lanka, I was shown rubies as big as my hand, and in **Maabar**, on the west coast of India, the finest pearls I'd ever seen.

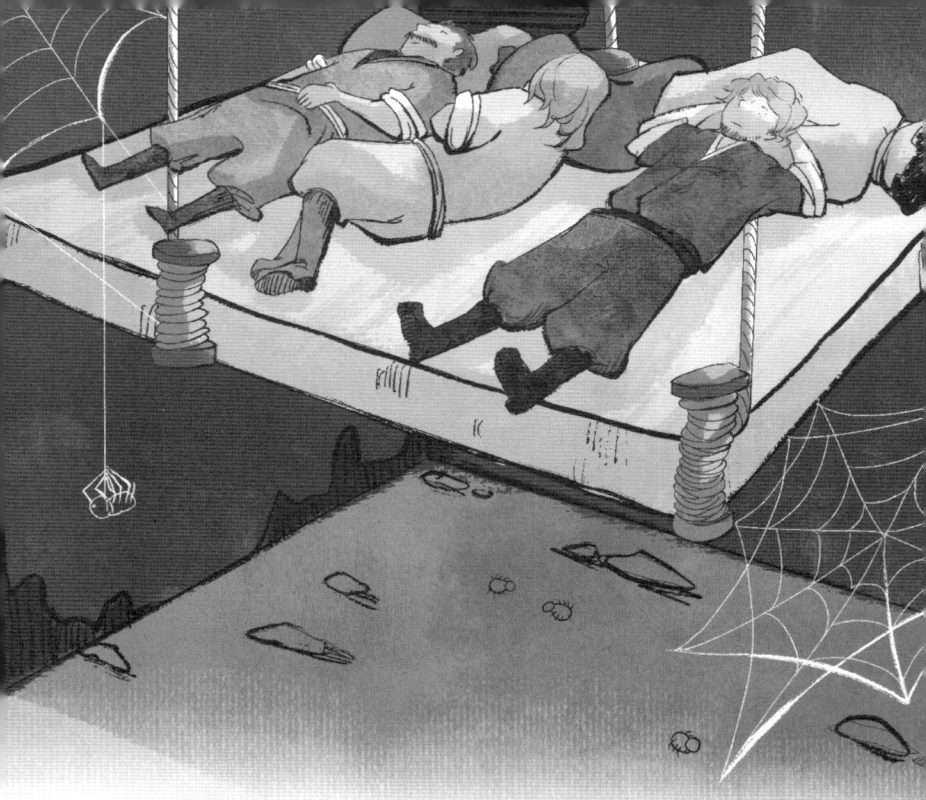

Everyone wore pearls there, but the most dazzling belonged to the king. They must have been worth the same as a small city – imagine wearing those around your neck. While I was there, I also checked out the region's rich, red soil, which was supposed to have healing properties. When no one was looking, I filled a small pot to take home with me. Before I knew it, my time in India was almost over. It was such a fascinating country, but there were two things about it I wouldn't miss – the heat and … the spiders.

Along the coast, the heat was terrible – I felt like I was being roasted alive, and the water in the rivers became hot enough to boil an egg. But the spiders were even worse – they had poisonous bites and lurked everywhere, ready to strike when you least expected. To get any sleep at all, we had to sleep in beds suspended on ropes close to the ceiling. Many merchants preferred to travel at night when it was cooler. They slept in their hanging beds during the day, using their bags of pearls and jewels as pillows.

When I arrived back in China, I was shocked to see that Kublai Khan was fading fast, making it ever more urgent we left for Venice, and soon. But first we had the tricky task of persuading the emperor to let us go. What would we do if he still said no? One day, my father caught the khan in a rare, good mood and seized his chance. Bowing deeply, he begged the emperor to grant our wish to go home and see our families. As expected, the khan flatly refused. My father tried again a few days later but the reply was the same.

I must confess I found myself feeling sorry for the khan. He was old, sick and grief-stricken, and wanted to keep his friends close. But just as it seemed like we'd come to a standstill, the emperor summoned us. He told us he needed someone he trusted to carry out an important mission – escorting a Mongol princess called Kököchin to Iran for her marriage to the king. That person had to be an experienced traveller, and he couldn't think of anyone better suited for the job than me! It helped that I was also an expert sailor (OK, so I may have exaggerated a bit), as we'd be travelling by sea to save the princess from the perils of journeying overland. My father and uncle would go with me, as long as we promised to return once we'd completed our task.

Eager to be off, we quickly agreed, although we had no intention of coming back. In my heart of hearts, I knew I'd never see the khan again. The year was 1292, and I was 38 years old. Impossible though it was to grasp, I was going home. Taking our leave of Kublai Khan was one of the hardest days of my life. He'd been such a hero to me and shown me so much love and care. As parting gifts, he gave us new gold paizas, stamped with the royal seal – I would treasure mine for ever.

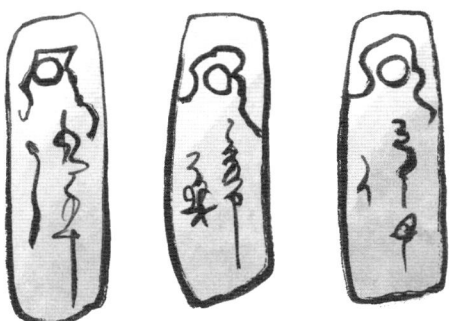

Then, it was time to join the mighty fleet he'd arranged for us – 14 magnificent ships, each with four masts and 12 sails, and carrying well over 1,000 passengers and crew. I couldn't wait to get on board.

Needless to say, the long voyage across the ocean wasn't all plain sailing. In fact, at times, it was so dreadful I don't know how we survived. We were rocked by storms, plagued by outbreaks of disease, some of our ships were wrecked and we were viciously attacked by pirates. By the time we reached Iran, almost two years later, more than 500 of the people who'd sailed from China had perished.

My father, uncle and I counted ourselves very lucky to be alive, as well as the princess, thank goodness, but we suffered another shock when we reached Persia – unbeknownst to us, the king was dead! Had we risked our lives for nothing? As it turned out, the princess married the king's son instead and everyone was happy, but we still couldn't get on our way. We ended up staying there for another nine months to help the princess settle into her new life because she was seriously homesick. I began to despair of ever seeing Venice again.

When we did, finally, set off, we travelled overland. For the first part of the journey, we had 100 horses and soldiers to guard us, but after that, we were left to fend for ourselves. By then, we were too far from China for the khan's paizas to count for much, so we fully expected some dangerous times to lie ahead. I still thought of the khan often and was dismayed when news reached us of his death. I vowed never to forget him but to repay his kindness by telling people what a truly great leader, and friend, he was.

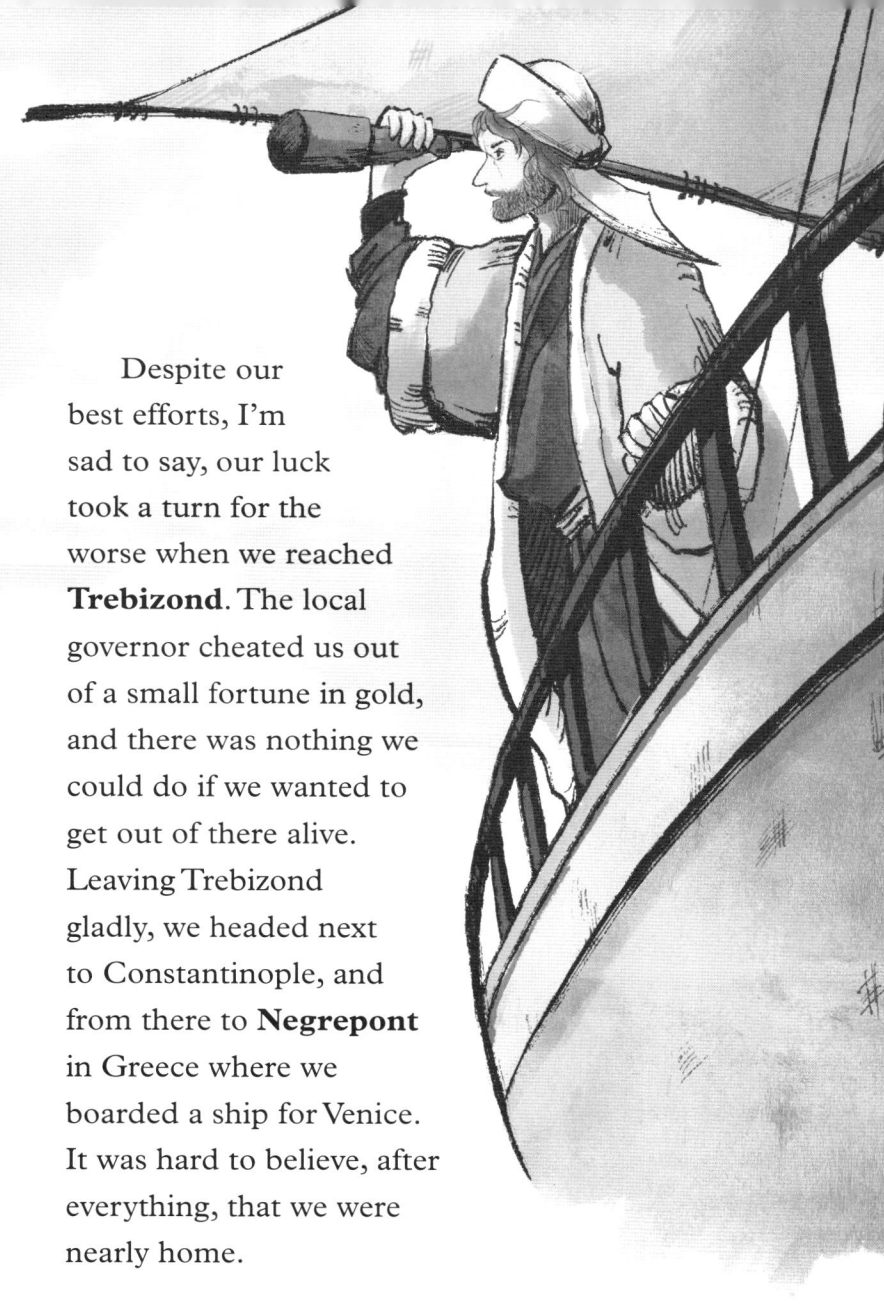

Despite our best efforts, I'm sad to say, our luck took a turn for the worse when we reached **Trebizond**. The local governor cheated us out of a small fortune in gold, and there was nothing we could do if we wanted to get out of there alive. Leaving Trebizond gladly, we headed next to Constantinople, and from there to **Negrepont** in Greece where we boarded a ship for Venice. It was hard to believe, after everything, that we were nearly home.

7. Taken prisoner

I don't know what I was expecting when I set foot on Venetian soil for the first time in so many years. If it was a warm welcome I was hoping for, I was in for a very big disappointment. Nobody even recognised us, let alone said how glad they were to see us back. And it got worse. When we knocked on the door of the Polo family home, they refused to let us in and wouldn't believe us when we told them our names. I don't suppose we could blame them for being suspicious. We were still wearing our Mongol clothes, which were, by then, woefully worn and ragged. In addition, our Venetian was rusty after so many years of speaking Mongolian. But even so, you'd have thought someone would be pleased to see us. Instead, it seemed, after 20 years, people had long ago given us up for dead.

I found being back in Venice very odd and unsettling and often wished I was back at Kublai Khan's court. So much of the city looked familiar, yet I felt like a stranger in my own home. Even my half-brother, Maffeo, had serious doubts about our true identities. We'd never met before, it's true – my father got married again last time he was home and Maffeo was born while we were away – but it meant our relationship got off to a rocky start. It wasn't the only one.

Not only did our strange outfits turn heads in the street, they nearly cost Uncle Maffeo his marriage. Although his wife was thrilled to have him home, she hated his Mongolian clothes. My uncle argued they were comfortable, and he was keeping them for old times' sake, and so my aunt took drastic action. She secretly bundled up the clothes and gave them away to a passing beggar. When she told my uncle what she'd done, he was beside himself. He spent days frantically searching the city until, eventually, he found the beggar and got his precious clothes back. I've never seen him look so relieved. For sewn into the linings of the robes was his entire collection of gems. They were worth a small fortune, and the beggar hadn't even noticed they were there.

Despite everything, my family still wasn't convinced we were who we said we were. My own family! It was time to settle the matter once and for all. So, we threw a magnificent feast for all of our relatives. And, while they sat down to eat, my father, uncle and I handed out gifts of precious silk and velvet. Then we put on a show of dazzling sapphires, diamonds and emeralds that we'd brought back from East Asia. It all worked perfectly. We knew it would. Money and possessions were everything in Venice. People only needed to see how rich you were, and they'd believe anything.

Not only did they accept us, they couldn't get enough of us. Every day, I'd get visitors turning up at my door, begging to hear more travel stories. I was only too pleased to oblige, of course. I loved nothing more than describing the wonderful things I'd seen in China –

paper money, eyeglasses, coal and gunpowder, for instance, which no one had heard of in Europe until our return. It was a joy to watch their mouths fall open in astonishment. People also asked to see my gold paiza, my most prized possession. When I looked at it, I remembered Kublai Khan and told them the remarkable story of his life.

Unfortunately, we'd timed our return at a difficult time for Venice. Political problems had been followed by years of famine, flooding and earthquakes. Life in the city was tough and grim. Then, war was declared between Venice and its arch-rival Genoa. The two cities competed with each other for trade and, despite a truce between them, the cracks began to show. In Venice, a call went out for people to join the war effort and, before I knew it, I found myself being drawn in. You could call my actions reckless but, after all the adventures we'd had, I missed the thrill of travelling and was finding the days dragged at home. That's how, in 1298, at the age of 43, I found myself fighting the **Genoese** at the Battle of **Curzola**. I was given command of a galley but, unfortunately, our fleet was quickly and roundly defeated and I was taken prisoner.

Being in prison wasn't as bad as it sounds, however. I had comfortable quarters and plenty to eat and, better still, it allowed me a much-needed break from all the hustle and bustle of life in Venice. I had time to sit back and let my mind wander back along the Silk Road, and I took full advantage of this. It was in prison that I met Rustichello da Pisa, an author of epic tales who agreed to write down my stories in a book – as you know, I'd kept notes of everything and was given permission to send for my notebooks to help jog my memory.

I hardly needed any reminding but Rustichello, who trained as a lawyer, wanted to see proof I was telling the truth. He decided the book should be written in French – the language of adventure. I couldn't really argue. While I spoke Mongolian, Persian and Venetian, of course, my French was non-existent. His wasn't brilliant either, I later learnt, and what he wrote was riddled with spelling mistakes.

Even so, he was doing me a favour and so every day, for many months, I dictated my stories to Rustichello and he wrote them down. Truth be told, if I hadn't been in prison, I'd never have sat still for so long. It was often tiring work, for him especially – while I could (and did) go on for hours, he could often be found nodding off to sleep. Still, we got along pretty well, even if he did tell me off for talking too fast. He was right. I had so much to say, it came out in a great, garbled rush and I didn't dare slow down in case I missed something out.

8. Family matters

While I was dictating away to Rustichello, my father and uncle had several goes at getting me out of prison by offering to pay a ransom. Part of the reason, I later found out, was that they wanted me to get married and, for that, I had to be home. Thank goodness, they didn't succeed. If they had, I'd never have had time to tell Rustichello everything. Happily, they didn't have too long to wait. In May 1299, peace was declared between Venice and Genoa, and Rustichello and I were set free. I made my way back to Venice, and that's where I stayed for the rest of my life. To my father and uncle's great relief, I finally felt ready to settle down.

My family continued to go up in the world and bought a splendid new house in a fashionable part of the city, complete with tower and courtyard. From then on, that's where I called home. With business doing so well, it wasn't long before I took my place in the Polo family firm. I was a proper merchant now – it's what I'd dreamt of as a young lad. I also got married. My new wife, Donato, was a merchant's daughter so she knew all about the world I came from. Over the years, we were blessed with three beautiful daughters and named them Fantina, Bellela and Moreta. Sadly, my father died but Uncle Maffeo was still going strong. With our travelling days well and truly behind us, we went into business together, and I never looked back. Anyway, now that I was a family man, I wanted to stick around.

As for my book, it became a bestseller, and I'm really not surprised. It was brilliant, if I do say so myself, and Rustichello turned out to be right about the French.

It had a number of titles, including *The Book of the Marvels of the World*. It was translated into many other European languages, including Venetian, and I carried copies with me wherever I went. I liked to hand them out to wealthy merchants and nobles who I knew would keep them safe in the libraries in their palatial homes. In 1310, dear Uncle Maffeo died. He never had children and, in his will, he left most of his enormous fortune to me and his other nephews. Soon afterwards, my half-brother, Maffeo, also passed away, leaving his estate to me, as well. I now controlled the largest share of the family business, though I missed my uncle terribly. He was the last person I really talked to about China.

By 1318, I'd become a grandfather. I couldn't wait for my grandchildren to hear about my travels when they're old enough. We all lived happily together in our big house, and my sons-in-law helped me with the business, taking my side in any quarrels with other family members. I was a very lucky man. As I approached 70, though, my health began to take a downward slide, and I found myself getting weaker day by day and having to spend most of my time in bed. Despite my family's reassurances, I only had to look at my doctor's face to see I didn't have long left to live.

So, one cold winter's day, I called for a lawyer to draw up my will. It won't surprise you to hear that I'd already put my affairs in order and decided who was going to get what. Over the years, I'd made a great deal of money so there was plenty to go around, and I also had property and valuables like fine cloth. Last but not least, there were my most treasured possessions – the precious objects I'd brought back from China all those years ago.

There was my golden paiza from Kublai Khan, which had seen me through so many hardships. There was a Buddhist rosary, made from boxwood, which reminded me of all the amazing Buddhist temples I'd seen, and the holy monks I'd met. And there was a gleaming Mongol helmet, exquisitely decorated with gems and pearls. It was a gift from the princess we'd escorted from China to Iran. All three meant the world to me. Looking at them, as I lay in my bed close to death, I was a young man once again, having the adventure of a lifetime. I found myself transported back to magical Quinsay, to Kublai Khan's court at Cambulac, and to the desperate wastes of the Gobi Desert – all the stuff of so many dreams. And to anyone who still doubts I've been telling the truth, I say, I haven't written down even half of the things I saw. If I had, no one would have believed a word.

Final word – journey's end

Marco Polo died on 8th or 9th January 1324 and was buried in the graveyard of the Church of San Lorenzo in Venice, close to his father, Niccolò. They had travelled the world together and it seemed fitting that they now shared a final resting place.

For years after Marco's death, and despite the detailed will he left, the Polo family continued to squabble about who owned which pieces of his gold, cloth, jewels and property. They paid very little attention to what Marco considered to be his greatest achievement – the book of his extraordinary travels. There were also some people who still doubted the truth of Marco's account.

Marco always said truth was stranger than fiction and knew it could be difficult for people to grasp, and he was proved right. We now know that most of what he described was not only true but also opened up the world to Europeans, as well as leading the way for other explorers to follow in his footsteps.

One of the most famous of these explorers was Christopher Columbus. In the late 15th and early 16th centuries, Columbus took a copy of Marco's book on all four of his voyages to the Americas while searching for a trade sea route to East Asia. In the margins, he made careful notes about spices and other valuable crops mentioned by Marco and which Columbus had dreams of trading. Unlike Marco, Columbus had not made it to East Asia but landed on islands in the Caribbean, and his voyages began Europe's long and violent colonisation of the Americas. Another explorer was Antonio Pigafetta who, like Marco, also came from Venice. In 1519, Pigafetta sailed with Ferdinand Magellan on his expedition to find a western route to East Asia, but resulted in the first known **circumnavigation** of the globe. Of about 270 men who set off, only 18 completed the voyage and returned home to Spain due to **mutiny**, **sabotage**, starvation, storms and violent encounters with **indigenous** peoples. Pigafetta was among them, but Magellan was not. Pigafetta spent the next few years writing a detailed account of the historic voyage, inspired by his great hero, Marco Polo.

Today, an incredible 700 years after his death, the name of Marco Polo is still known all over the world. People are fascinated by his intrepid travels and continue to marvel at the incredible journey undertaken by a teenager from Venice who dreamt of becoming a merchant but had never been away from home before.

Glossary of places

Acre port city, northern Israel

Cambulac modern-day Beijing, China

Constantinople modern-day Istanbul, Turkey

Curzola modern-day Korčula, a Croatian island in the Adriatic Sea

Holy Land in the 13th century, this was an area that included Israel, the West Bank and Gaza, Lebanon, western Jordan and south-west Syria

Hormuz modern-day Hormuz Island, off the coast of southern Iran

Khotan modern-day Hotan, north-west China

Lop modern-day Lop Nur, north-west China

Maabar modern-day Tamil Nadu, southern India

Negrepont Italian name for Euboea, a Greek island in the Aegean Sea

Pamir Mountains a mountain range between Central and South Asia

Quinsay modern-day Hangzhou, eastern China

Silk Road network of interconnected land and sea trade routes linking East Asia with the Middle East and Europe

Tauris modern-day Tabriz, Iran

Trebizond modern-day Trabzon, northern Turkey

Glossary

caravanserai a guest house with a central courtyard

circumnavigation travel all the way around (something)

galleys ships with one or more sails and up to three rows of oars

Genghis Khan warrior-ruler who founded the Mongol Empire

Genoese people from the Italian city of Genoa

gorging filling oneself with food; overeating

indigenous people inhabiting land before the arrival of colonialists

khan a title meaning emperor, used in the Mongol Empire, and usually added to a name, for example, Kublai Khan

mutiny when people refuse to obey the orders of someone in charge

nomads people who travel from place to place to find fresh pasture for animals

oasis a spot in the desert where water is found

royal seal a symbol or emblem showing the authority of a monarch

sabotage deliberately destroy or damage something

thinning air a term used to describe when there's less oxygen in the air, which makes it more difficult to breathe

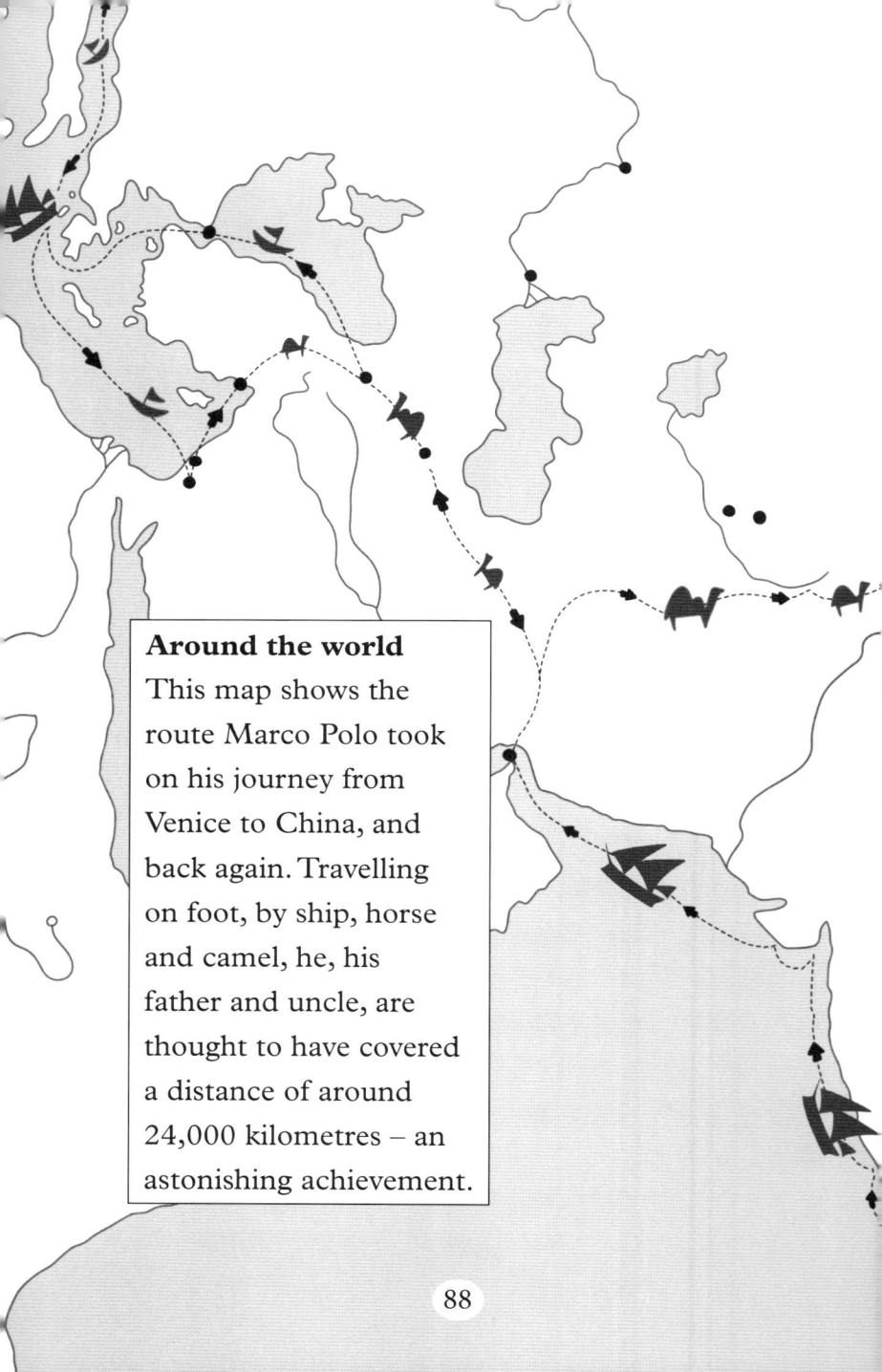

Around the world

This map shows the route Marco Polo took on his journey from Venice to China, and back again. Travelling on foot, by ship, horse and camel, he, his father and uncle, are thought to have covered a distance of around 24,000 kilometres – an astonishing achievement.

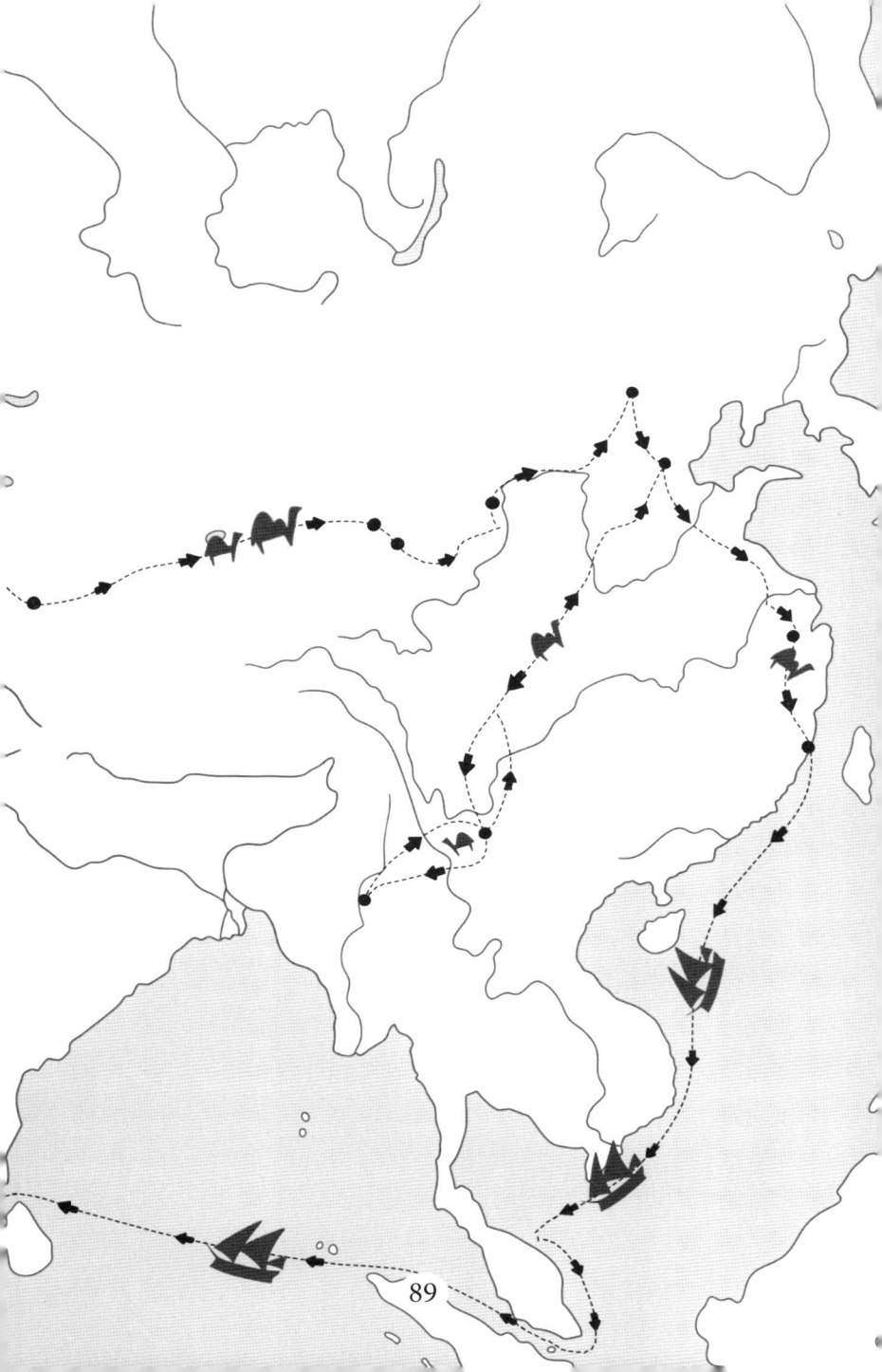

Book talk questions

Had you ever heard of Marco Polo before reading this book? What did you learn about him?

Of all the places he went to, which one did you find the most interesting?

If you could travel the world, where would you choose to go and why?

What do you think are the pros and cons of travelling?

Why do you think some people didn't believe Marco Polo's stories?

Who is your favourite figure from the book?

What do you think is the most important lesson Marco Polo learnt during his travels?

If you could write a letter to Marco Polo, what would you tell him about your life today?

In what ways did Marco Polo's stories change the way people viewed the world?

How different would Marco Polo's experiences be if he was alive today?

Ask the author

Is there a particular moment or story about Marco Polo's life that sparked your interest the most?

His childhood in Venice. It must have been an extraordinary place to grow up in. I was lucky enough to visit Venice a few years ago and see the Polos' house by the Grand Canal.

Anita Ganeri

What kind of research did you do to accurately portray Marco Polo's adventures?

I mostly read lots of books, including an edition of *The Travels of Marco Polo*.

What message do you hope readers will get from this book?

I hope it encourages readers to take an interest in the wider world. I love to travel and consider it one of the most rewarding experiences of my life.

What was the biggest challenge writing this book?

Trying to fit everything in – it is such a fascinating story and there is so much to say. I had to be very strict with myself.

Are there any other historical figures or events you're interested in writing about in the future?
Yes, lots of other explorers, including women like Mary Kingsley. She lived in Victorian times when women weren't expected to travel, but she set off for Africa nonetheless.

What is the most interesting place you have ever travelled to?
Uzbekistan – one of the countries on the Silk Road. It was absolutely amazing.

If you could ask Marco Polo a question, what would it be?
The same question – what is the most interesting place you have ever travelled to?

What other adventure stories would you recommend?
Any stories about polar adventurers, such as Amundsen and Scott, or Shackleton, who diced with death to explore the most perilous places on Earth.

Published by Collins
An imprint of HarperCollins*Publishers*

The News Building
1 London Bridge Street
London SE1 9GF
UK

Macken House
39/40 Mayor Street Upper
Dublin 1
D01 C9W8
Ireland

© HarperCollins*Publishers* Limited 2026

10 9 8 7 6 5 4 3 2 1

ISBN 978-0-00-878479-9

All rights reserved. No part of this publication may be reproduced, stored in a retrieval system, or transmitted in any form by any means, electronic, mechanical, photocopying, recording or otherwise, without the prior written permission of the Publisher or a licence permitting restricted copying in the United Kingdom issued by the Copyright Licensing Agency Ltd, 5th Floor, Shackleton House, 4 Battle Bridge Lane, London SE1 2HX.

Without limiting the exclusive rights of any author, contributor or the publisher of this publication, any unauthorised use of this publication to train generative artificial intelligence (AI) technologies is expressly prohibited. HarperCollins also exercise their rights under Article 4(3) of the Digital Single Market Directive 2019/790 and expressly reserve this publication from the text and data mining exception.

British Library Cataloguing-in-Publication Data
A catalogue record for this publication is available from the British Library.

Author: Anita Ganeri
Illustrator: Pino Cao (Illo Agency)
Publisher: Laura White
Commissioning editor: Holly Woolnough
Development editor: Zoë Clarke
Product manager: Holly Woolnough
Content editor: Selin Akca
Copyeditor: Sally Byford

Proofreader: Tanya Solomons
Reviewer: Lisa Davis
Fact checker: Sasha Morton
Cover designer: Sarah Finan
Internal designer: 2Hoots Publishing Services Ltd
Typesetter: David Jimenez
Production controller: Sophie Waeland

Collins would like to thank the teachers and children at Grange Primary School, Southwark, for being part of the development of Big Cat Read On.

Printed in the UK

Made with responsibly sourced paper and vegetable ink

Scan to see how we are reducing our environmental impact.

Get the latest Collins Big Cat news at
collins.co.uk/collinsbigcat